HOW TO DRAW FOR MINECRAFTERS

A STEP BY STEP EASY GUIDE

Do you want to learn how to draw Minecraft stuff?

This guide will show you how to draw 50 different mobs, tools and other stuff from Minecraft starting from scratch to its final details. Some of the characters and items are easy to draw and some are a little challenging, but as you will discover in the book everything starts from squares and lines. So as long as you can draw squares, circles and lines you'll be able to draw these awesome stuff.

So what are you waiting for?
    1. Sharpen your pencil
    2. Get your paper
    3. Have an eraser too to erase errors and to remove line guides
    4. Grab your crayons so you can also color your masterpiece
    5. and last of all Have fun!!!

STEVE

DIFFICULTY LEVEL

1 FIRST DRAW THE SHAPE OF STEVE'S HEAD AND TORSO.

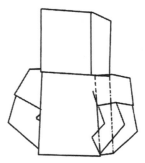

2 DRAW HIS HANDS. ERASE DOTTED LINES.

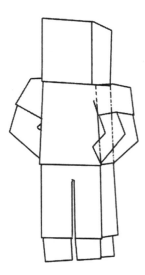

3 NEXT STEP IS EASY JUST FOLLOW OUR LEAD. DRAW HIS LEGS.

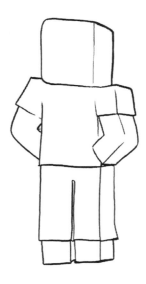

4 ALMOST DONE! NOW WHEN YOU HAVE THE SHAPE OF STEVE'S BODY USE THICKER LINES TO DRAW HIS FINAL SHAPE.

5 FEW MORE DETAILS AND OUR STEVE IS DONE! ADD HIM A FACE, SOME SHADING AND HE IS READY.

Now, it's your turn

CREEPER

DIFFICULTY LEVEL

1 FIRST DRAW THE SHAPE OF A CREEPER'S HEAD.

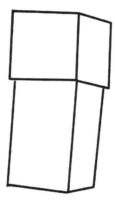

2 DRAW A RECTANGULAR CUBOID BELOW HIS HEAD TO CREATE HIS TORSO.

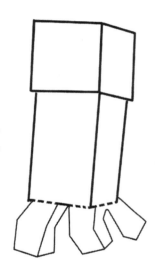

3 NEXT DRAW HIS LEGS.

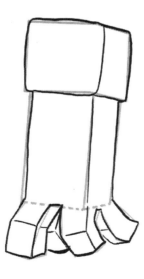

4 ALMOST DONE! NOW WHEN YOU HAVE THE SHAPE OF THE CREEPER USE THICKER LINES TO DRAW HIS FINAL SHAPE.

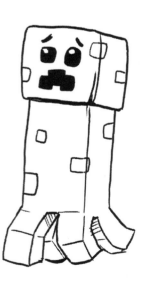

5 FEW MORE DETAILS AND OUR CREEPER IS DONE! ADD HIM A FACE, SOME SPOTS AND HE IS DONE.

Now, it's your turn

ALEX

DIFFICULTY LEVEL

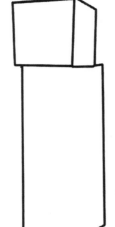

1 START WITH DRAWING THE SHAPE OF ALEX'S HEAD AND TORSO.

2 DRAW HER HANDS. ERASE DOTTED LINES.

3 NEXT STEP IS EASY. JUST FOLLOW OUR LEAD AND DRAW HER LEGS.

4 ALMOST DONE! NOW WHEN YOU HAVE THE SHAPE OF ALEX USE THICKER LINES TO DRAW HER FINAL SHAPE. DRAW ALEX'S FACE AND SOME LINES FOR SHADINGS.

Now, it's your turn

BAT

DIFFICULTY LEVEL

1 START WITH DRAWING THE SHAPE OF THE BAT'S HEAD AND TORSO.

2 THEN DRAW HIS WINGS AND EARS. ERASE DOTTED LINES.

3 NEXT STEP IS EASY. JUST FOLLOW OUR GUIDELINES FOR HIS BODY.

4 ALMOST DONE! NOW WHEN YOU HAVE THE SHAPE OF THE BAT USE THICKER LINES TO DRAW HIS FINAL SHAPE. DRAW THE BAT'S FACE AND SOME LINES FOR SHADINGS.

Now, it's your turn

Now, it's your turn

CHICKEN

DIFFICULTY LEVEL

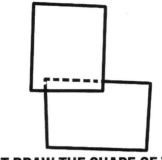

1 FIRST DRAW THE SHAPE OF THE CHICKEN'S HEAD AND TORSO.

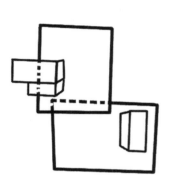

2 NOW DRAW ITS BEAK AND WING ERASE DOTTED LINES.

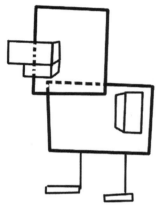

3 NEXT STEP IS EASY. JUST FOLLOW OUR LEAD AND DRAW ITS LEGS.

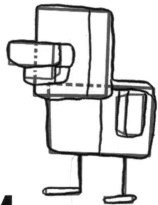

4 ALMOST DONE! NOW WHEN YOU HAVE THE SHAPE OF THE CHICKEN USE THICKER LINES TO DRAW HIS FINAL SHAPE.

5 FEW MORE DETAILS AND OUR CHICKEN IS DONE! ADD ITS FACE, SOME SHADING AND IT IS DONE.

Now, it's your turn

RABBIT

DIFFICULTY LEVEL

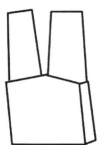

1 DRAW THE SHAPE OF THE RABBIT'S HEAD AND EARS.

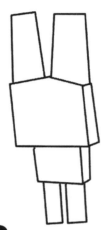

2 DRAW HIS TORSO AND HIS FRONT LEGS.

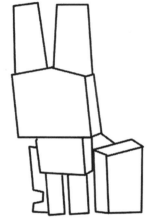

3 NEXT STEP IS EASY, DRAW HIS BACK LEGS.

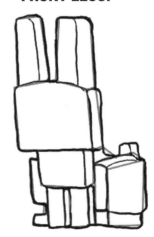

4 ALMOST DONE! NOW YOU HAVE THE SHAPE OF THE RABBIT.

5 DRAW THE RABBIT'S FACE. ADD A FEW MORE DETAILS AND SHADING AND OUR RABBIT IS DONE.

Now, it's your turn

COW

DIFFICULTY LEVEL

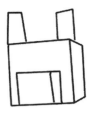

1 START WITH DRAWING THE COW'S HEAD AND EARS.

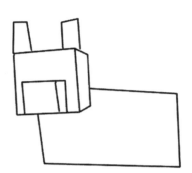

2 NOW DRAW COW'S TORSO

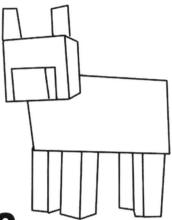

3 NEXT STEP IS TO DRAW ITS LEGS

4 ALMOST DONE! TRACE WITH THICKER LINES THE FINAL SHAPE OF THE COW

5 DRAW ITS FACE. ADD A FEW MORE DETAILS LIKE SPOTS, TAIL AND SOME SHADING.

Now, it's your turn

TULIP

DIFFICULTY LEVEL

1 FIRST DRAW A STEM.

2 NEXT DRAW THE SHAPE OF THE FLOWER.

3 ADD SOME LEAVES.

4 NOW ADD MORE LEAVES TO OUR PLANT'S STEM.

5 ADD FEW MORE DETAILS TO BRING OUR TULIP TO LIFE AND ITS DONE.

Now, it's your turn

SHEEP

DIFFICULTY LEVEL

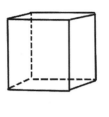
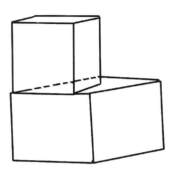

1 FIRST DRAW THE SHAPE OF THE SHEEP'S HEAD.

2 ADD LEGS AND SHEEP'S TAIL

3 ALMOST DONE, NOW YOU HAVE THE SHAPE OF THE SHEEP.

4 ADD FACE FEATURES, EARS AND SOME SHADING AND YOU ARE DONE.

Now, it's your turn

MOOSHROOM

DIFFICULTY LEVEL

1 FIRST DRAW CUBE FOR MOOSHROOM'S HEAD AND ADD ITS EARS AND SNOUT.

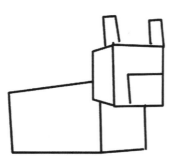

2 NEXT DRAW ITS TORSO

3 ADD ITS LEGS

4 ALMOST DONE, DRAW ITS TAIL

5 ADD FACE FEATURES, SPOTS, MUSHROOMS, AND SOME SHADING AND YOU ARE DONE.

Now, it's your turn

SQUID

DIFFICULTY LEVEL

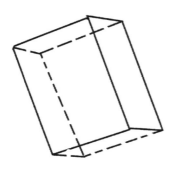

1 FIRST DRAW THIS SHAPE FOR SQUID'S HEAD.

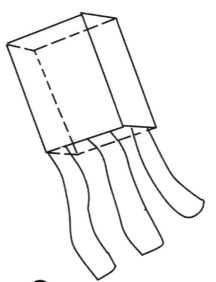

2 NOW ADD A FEW TENTACLES

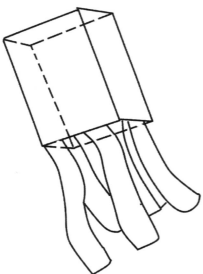

3 ADD MORE TENTACLES AND ERASE DOTTED LINES

4 ALMOST DONE, NOW YOU HAVE THE SHAPE OF THE SQUID, ADD ITS FACE FEATURES AND SOME SHADING AND THAT IS IT.

Now, it's your turn

SPIDER

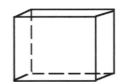

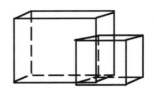

DIFFICULTY LEVEL

1 START WITH A CUBOID. DRAW A SMALLER CUBE BESIDE IT AS SHOWN IN THE IMAGE.

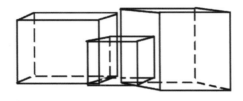

2 NEXT DRAW ANOTHER BIGGER CUBE ON THE OTHER SIDE OF THE SMALLER CUBE TO COMPLETE THE SPIDER'S BODY.

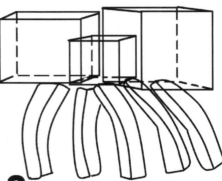

3 ADD LEGS TO OUR SPIDER'S BODY AND ERASE DOTTED LINES.

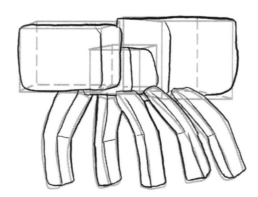

4 ALMOST DONE, NOW YOU HAVE THE SHAPE OF THE SPIDER.

5 ADD FACE FEATURES AND SOME SHADING AND YOU ARE DONE.

Now, it's your turn

Now, it's your turn

SLIME

DIFFICULTY LEVEL

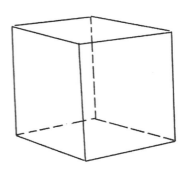

1 FIRST DRAW A CUBE

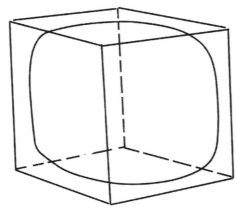

2 NEXT DRAW THIS SHAPE WHITIN THE CUBE.

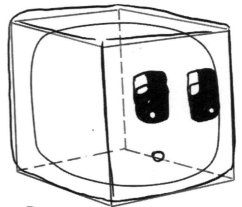

3 ADD HIS FACE AND ERASE DOTTED LINES

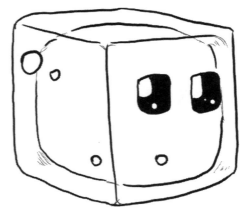

4 ALMOST DONE, NOW JUST ADD SOME FINAL DETAILS.

Now, it's your turn

ENDERMAN

DIFFICULTY LEVEL

1 FIRST DRAW A CUBE FOR THE ENDERMAN'S HEAD AND ADD HIS TORSO.

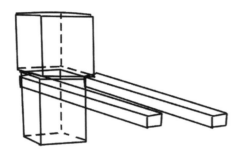

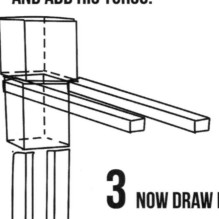

2 NEXT DRAW HIS HANDS LIKE THIS.

3 NOW DRAW HIS LEGS.

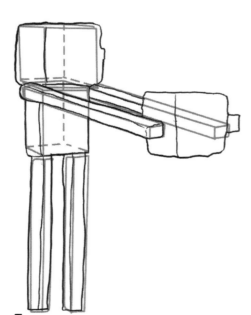

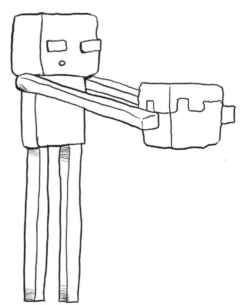

4 ALMOST DONE, DRAW A BLOCK BETWEEN THE HANDS OF THE ENDERMAN

5 ADD FACE FEATURES, SOME DETAILS, SOME SHADING AND YOU ARE DONE.

Now, it's your turn

GHAST

DIFFICULTY LEVEL

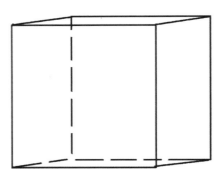

1 FIRST DRAW CUBE FOR GHAST'S BODY

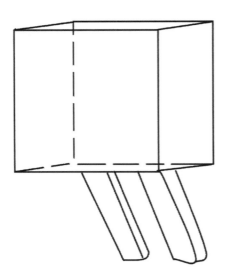

2 NEXT DRAW A FEW TENTACLES

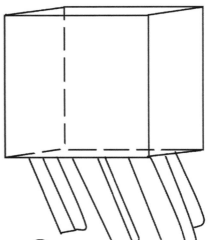

3 ADD MORE TENTACLES AND ERASE DOTTED LINES

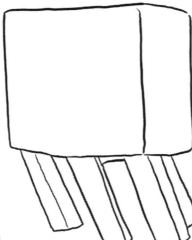

4 ALMOST DONE, NOW YOU HAVE THE SHAPE OF THE GHAST

5 ADD FACE FEATURES, SOME DETAILS AND SOME SHADING AND YOU ARE DONE.

Now, it's your turn

SNOW GOLEM

DIFFICULTY LEVEL

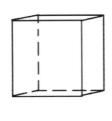 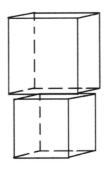

1 FIRST DRAW CUBE FOR HIS HEAD AND ANOTHER ONE FOR HIS TORSO.

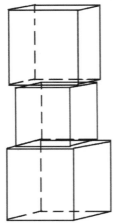

2 NEXT DRAW ANOTHER CUBE TO GET HIS FULL BODY SHAPE .

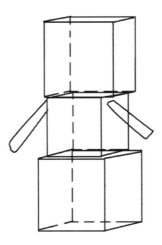

3 ADD HIS ARMS AND ERASE DOTTED LINES.

4 ALMOST DONE, NOW DRAW HIS FACE.

5 ADD MORE DETAILS AND SOME SHADING AND YOU ARE DONE.

Now, it's your turn

ENDER DRAGON

DIFFICULTY LEVEL

1 FIRST DRAW A CUBE FOR HIS HEAD AND ADD HIS EARS AND SNOUT.

2 NEXT DRAW TORSO, NECK AND TAIL LIKE THIS.

3 NEXT, ADD HIS LEGS.

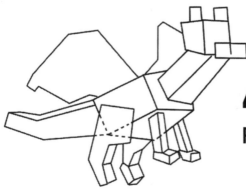

4 ALMOST DONE, NOW DRAW HIS WINGS FOLLOWING THIS

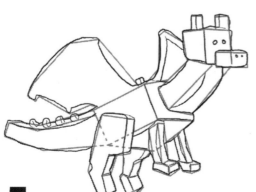

5 ADD FACE FEATURES, ERASE DOTTED LINES AND YOU HAVE MAIN SHAPE OF OUR DRAGON.

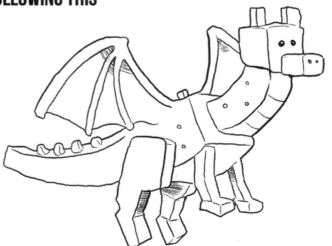

6 ADD SOME MORE DETAILS AND SOME SHADING AND YOU ARE DONE.

Now, it's your turn

BOW AND ARROW

DIFFICULTY LEVEL

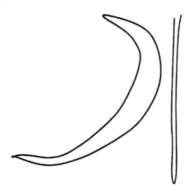

1 FIRST DRAW MAIN SHAPE OF BOW AND LINE FOR ARROW.

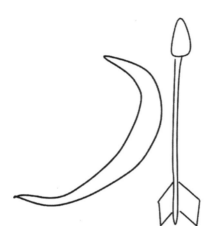

2 NEXT DRAW THESE SHAPES FOR ARROW.

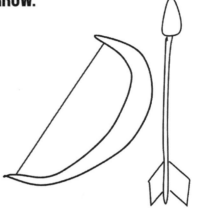

3 ADD A LINE FOR BOW'S STRING.

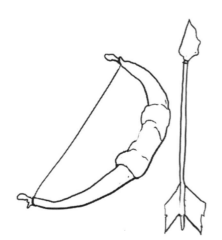

4 ALMOST DONE, NOW DRAW SOME DETAILS.

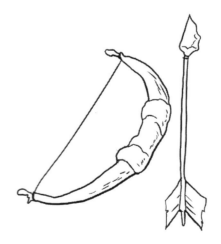

5 ADD FEW DETAILS AND SOME SHADING AND YOU ARE DONE.

Now, it's your turn

SWORD

DIFFICULTY LEVEL

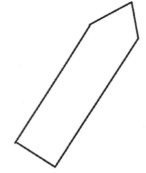

1 FIRST DRAW THIS SHAPE FOR BLADE

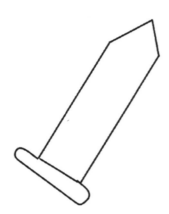

2 NEXT DRAW THIS SHAPE

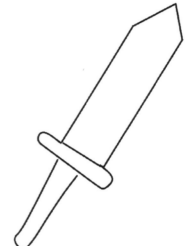

3 NEXT ADD THIS SHAPE FOR HANDLE

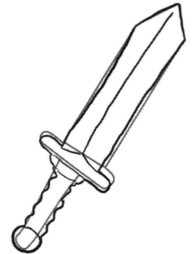

4 ALMOST DONE, NOW YOU HAVE THE MAIN SHAPE OF THE SWORD.

5 ADD SOME DETAILS AND SHADING LINES AND YOU ARE DONE.

Now, it's your turn

AXE

DIFFICULTY LEVEL

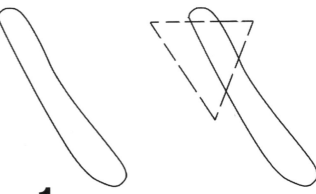

1 FIRST DRAW THIS SHAPE FOR AXE'S HANDLE AND DRAW A TRIANGLE.

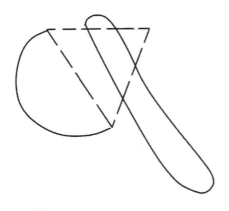

2 NEXT DRAW THIS SHAPE TO HAVE THE BLADE PART OF THE AXE.

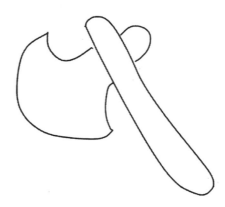

3 FOLLOW THE SHAPE ABOVE AND REMOVE THE EXCESS LINES.

4 ALMOST DONE, NOW YOU HAVE MAIN SHAPE OF AXE

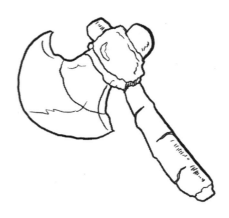

5 ADD SOME DETAILS, LINES AND SOME SHADING AND YOU ARE DONE.

Now, it's your turn

GUARDIAN

DIFFICULTY LEVEL

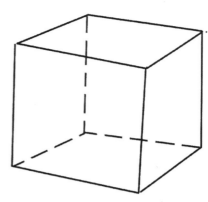

1 FIRST DRAW CUBE FOR GUARDIAN'S HEAD.

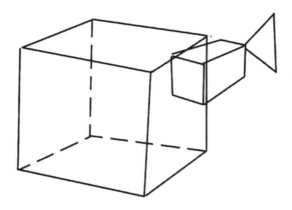

2 NEXT DRAW THESE SHAPES FOR HIS TAIL AND FIN

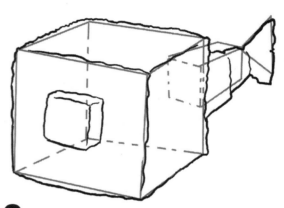

3 ADD A SMALL CUBE FOR HIS EYE

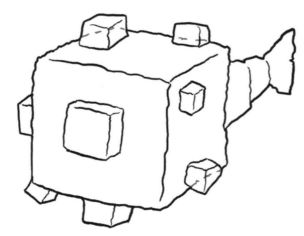

4 ALMOST DONE, NOW DRAW FEW MORE CUBE SHAPES FOR BUMPS ON HIS BODY

5 ADD DETAILS FOR HIS EYE, SOME LINES, SOME SHADING AND THAT IS IT

Now, it's your turn

WITHER

DIFFICULTY LEVEL

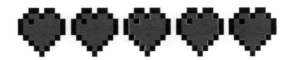

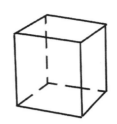

1 FIRST DRAW CUBE FOR WITHER'S HEAD.

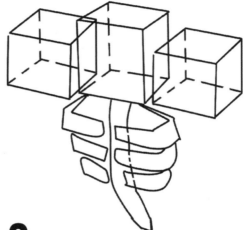

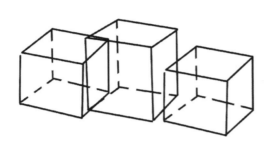

2 ADD TWO MORE CUBES

3 NEXT DRAW LINES FOR HIS BODY TO GET THIS SHAPE LIKE THIS

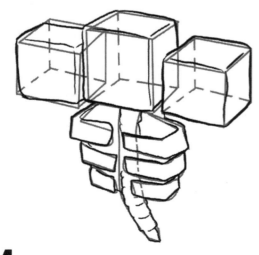

4 ALMOST DONE! NOW YOU HAVE THE MAIN SHAPE OF THE WITHER. ERASE DOTTED LINES.

5 ADD FACE FEATURES, SOME DETAILS SOME SHADING AND OUR WITHER IS DONE.

Now, it's your turn

IRON GOLEM

DIFFICULTY LEVEL

1 FIRST DRAW THIS SHAPE FOR GOLEM'S HEAD AND DRAW HIS TORSO.

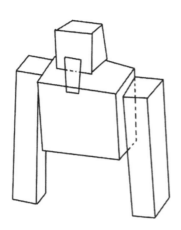

2 ADD HIS ARMS AS SHOWN IN THE IMAGE.

3 THEN ADD LOWER PART OF HIS BODY AND LEGS.

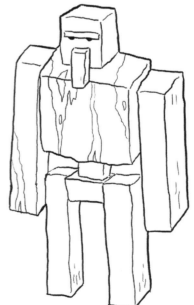

4 ALMOST DONE, DRAW HIS FACE AND ERASE DOTTED LINES AND NOW YOU HAVE THE SHAPE OF THE GOLEM.

5 ADD SOME LINES FOR TEXTURE AND SOME SHADING AND THAT IS IT..

Now, it's your turn

OCELOT

DIFFICULTY LEVEL

1 FIRST, DRAW A CUBE FOR THE OCELOT'S HEAD.

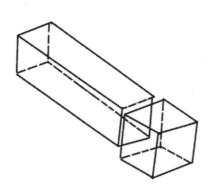

2 NEXT DRAW THIS SHAPE FOR ITS TORSO

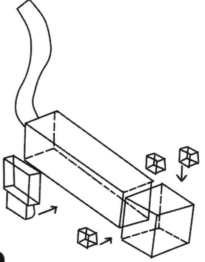

3 ADD LEGS, EARS AND OCELOT'S TAIL.

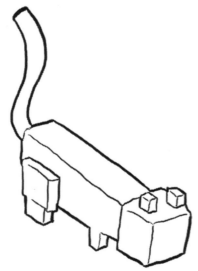

4 ALMOST DONE, ERASE DOTTED LINES AND NOW WE HAVE MAIN SHAPE OF OCELOT

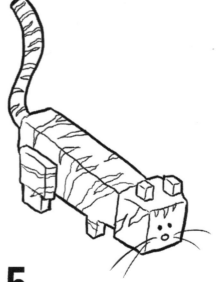

5 ADD FACE FEATURES, LINES AND SOME SHADING AND YOU ARE DONE.

Now, it's your turn

LLAMA

DIFFICULTY LEVEL

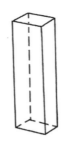 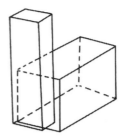

1 FIRST DRAW THE SHAPE OF THE LLAMA'S BODY.

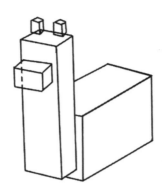

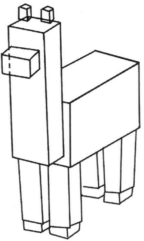

2 NEXT ERASE DOTTED LINES AND ADD EARS AND SNOUT

3 NOW ADD LLAMA'S LEGS.

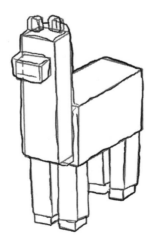

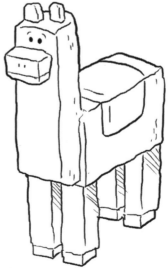

4 ALMOST DONE, NOW YOU HAVE THE SHAPE OF THE LLAMA.

5 ADD FACE FEATURES, ITS SADDLE AND SOME SHADING AND YOU ARE DONE.

Now, it's your turn

Now, it's your turn

HORSE

DIFFICULTY LEVEL

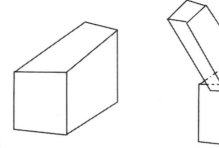

1 FIRST DRAW THESE SHAPES FOR HIS NECK AND BODY.

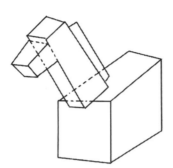

2 NEXT DRAW FEW MORE SHAPES FOR HORSE'S SNOUT AND MANE.

3 ADD LEGS AND HORSE'S TAIL

4 ALMOST DONE, NOW YOU HAVE THE SHAPE OF THE HORSE AND ERASE DOTTED LINES.

5 ADD FACE FEATURES, ITS SADDLE AND SOME SHADING AND YOU ARE DONE.

Now, it's your turn

LILAC

DIFFICULTY LEVEL

1 FIRST DRAW STEM OF LILAC.

2 ADD FLOWERS TO OUR PLANT.

3 ALMOST DONE, NOW ADD SOME LEAVES.

4 ADD FEW MORE DETAILS TO BRING OUR PLANT TO LIFE AND THAT IS IT.

Now, it's your turn

SKELETON

DIFFICULTY LEVEL

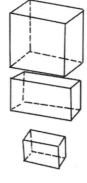

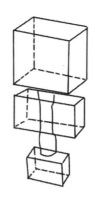

1 FIRST DRAW CUBIC SHAPES FOR HIS HEAD AND BODY

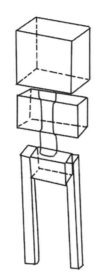

2 DRAW HIS LEGS.

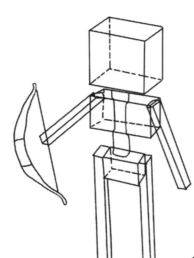

3 NEXT STEP IS TO ADD HIS HANDS AND A BOW ERASE DOTTED LINES

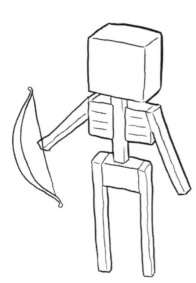

4 ALMOST DONE! NOW WHEN YOU HAVE A SHAPE OF SKELETON'S BODY USE THICKER LINES TO DRAW HIS FINAL SHAPE.

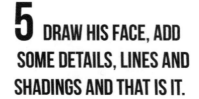

5 DRAW HIS FACE, ADD SOME DETAILS, LINES AND SHADINGS AND THAT IS IT.

Now, it's your turn

VILLAGER

DIFFICULTY LEVEL

1 FIRST DRAW THE SHAPE OF A VILLAGER'S HEAD.

2 ADD HIS ARMS.

3 NEXT STEP IS EASY. JUST FOLLOW OUR LEAD AND DRAW HIS TORSO

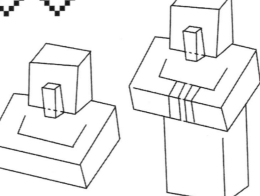

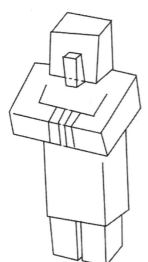

4 NOW JUST ADD HIS LEGS

5 ALMOST DONE. NOW DRAW HIS FACE FEATURES

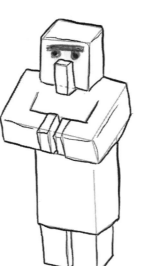

6 FEW MORE DETAILS AND SOME SHADING AND OUR VILLAGER IS DONE.

Now, it's your turn

CHEST

DIFFICULTY LEVEL

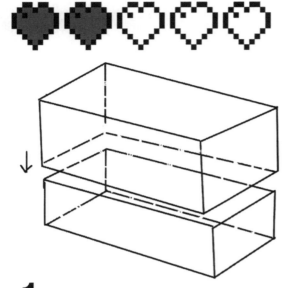

1 DRAW TWO CUBOID AS SHOWN

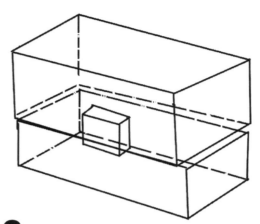

2 NOW DRAW A SMALL CUBOID FOR KEY HOLE. ERASE DOTTED LINES.

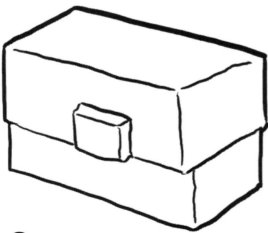

3 ALMOST DONE, NOW WE HAVE SHAPE OF CHEST

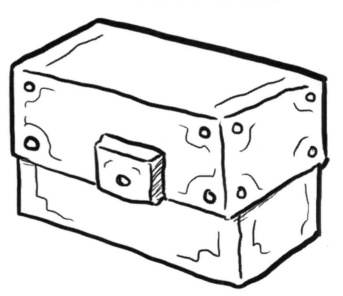

4 TO FINISH ADD SOME DETAILS AND SOME SHADING AND THAT IS IT.

Now, it's your turn

FURNACE

DIFFICULTY LEVEL

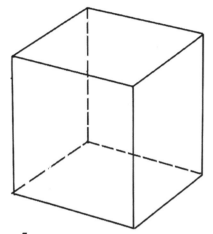

1 DRAW A CUBE LIKE THIS.

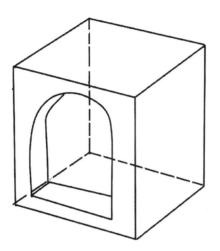

2 NOW DRAW SHAPE LIKE THIS ONE FOR FIRE HOLE, ERASE DOTTED LINES.

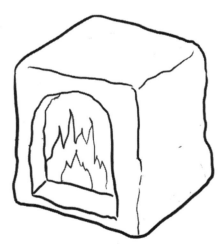

3 ALMOST DONE, NOW ADD SOME FLAMES INSIDE OUR SHAPE.

4 ADD SOME SHAPES FOR STONES, AND SOME MORE DETAILS LIKE THIS AND YOU ARE DONE.

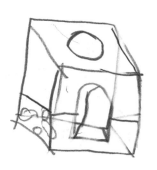

ANVIL

DIFFICULTY LEVEL

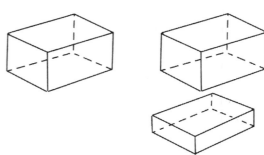

1 FIRST DRAW CUBOIDS LIKE THIS.

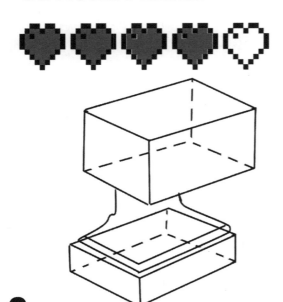

2 NEXT CONNECT THE TWO CUBOIDS AS SHOWN.

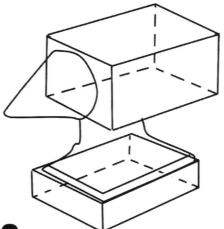

3 DRAW A CONE SHAPE ON THE UPPER CUBOID.

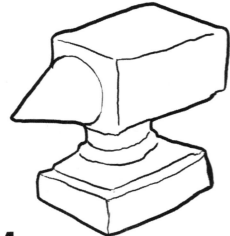

4 ALMOST DONE NOW YOU HAVE THE SHAPE OF THE ANVIL.

5 ADD SOME MORE LINES, SHADINGS AND DETAILS ON YOUR ANVIL TO FINISH THE DRAWING.

Now, it's your turn

MAGMA CUBE

DIFFICULTY LEVEL

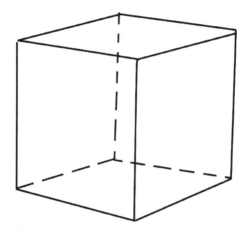

1 DRAW A CUBE.

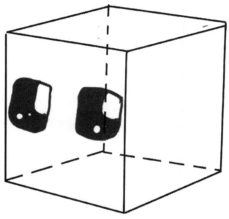

2 NOW DRAW ITS EYES LIKE THIS.

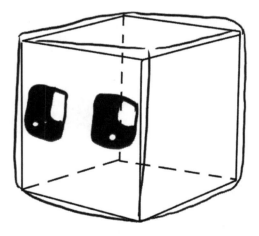

3 MAKE EDGES SOFTER LIKE THIS AND ERASE DOTTED LINES.

4 ALMOST DONE, JUST ADD SOME ROUND SHAPES FOR DETAILS AND YOU ARE DONE.

Now, it's your turn

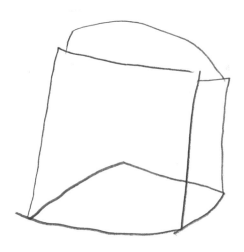

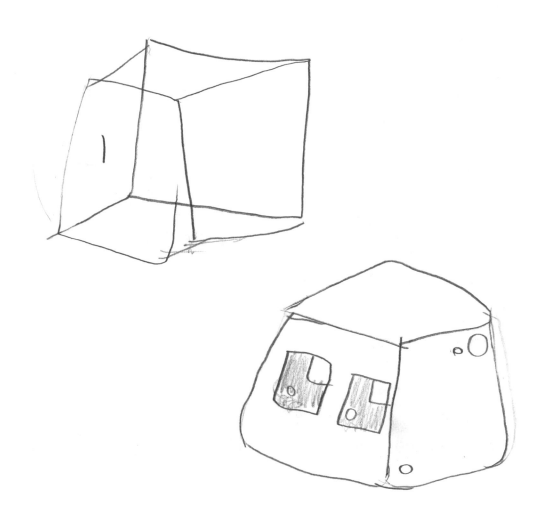

SUNFLOWER

DIFFICULTY LEVEL

1 DRAW STEM AND SHAPE OF OUR SUNFLOWER.

2 NOW DRAW ITS LEAVES ON STEM.

3 ALMOST DONE NOW ADD SOME SMALLER PETALS IN THE CENTER OF FLOWER.

4 ADD FEW MORE DETAILS AND OUR SUNFLOWER IS DONE.

Now, it's your turn

PICKAXE

DIFFICULTY LEVEL

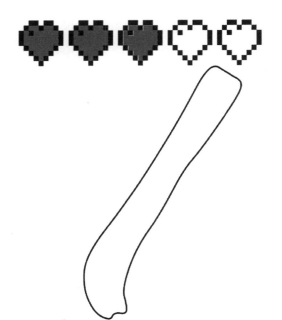

1 DRAW HANDLE SHAPE

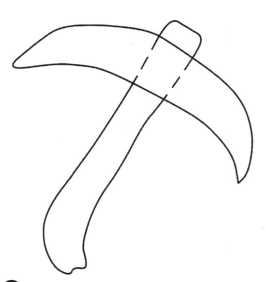

2 NEXT DRAW THIS SHAPE FOR TOP PART OF OUR PICKAXE

3 ALMOST DONE, ADD SOME LINES FOR ROPE

4 ADD SOME MORE LINES AND DETAILS ON THE HANDLE PART FOR WOOD TEXTURE AND WE ARE DONE.

Now, it's your turn

ARMOR STAND

DIFFICULTY LEVEL

1 DRAW THE SHAPE OF AN ARMOR.

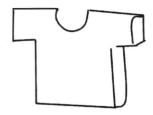

2 DRAW A STAND FOLLOWING THE IMAGE ABOVE.

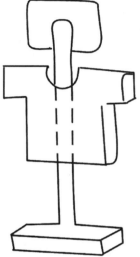

3 NOW DRAW A HELMET.

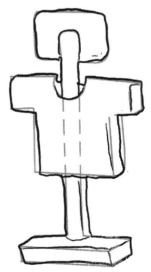

4 FOLLOW LINE GUIDES AND TRACE THE FINAL SHAPE. ERASE ALL LINE GUIDES.

5 TO MAKE IT MORE REALISTIC, USE THIN LINES FOR SMALL DETAILS AND SHADING.

Now, it's your turn

BOAT

DIFFICULTY LEVEL

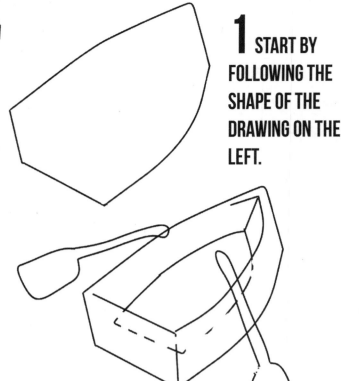

1 START BY FOLLOWING THE SHAPE OF THE DRAWING ON THE LEFT.

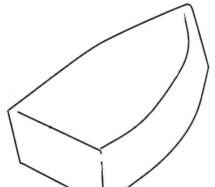

2 FOLLOW OUR DRAWING AND DRAW A SHAPE OF A BOAT.

3 NOW, DRAW THE BOTTOM PART OF THE BOAT AND 2 PADDLES.

4 FOLLOW THE LINE GUIDES AND TRACE THE FINAL SHAPE OF THE BOAT AND DRAW THE BOAT'S SITTING BENCH.

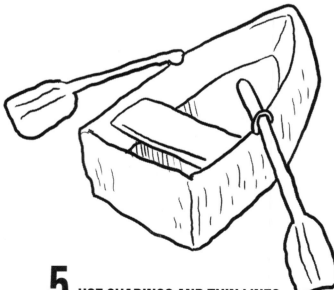

5 USE SHADINGS AND THIN LINES TO FINISH YOUR DRAWING.

Now, it's your turn

COMPASS

DIFFICULTY LEVEL

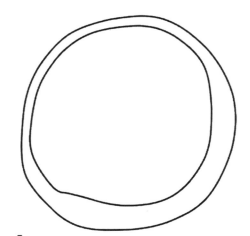

1 DRAW TWO CIRCLES, ONE INSIDE ANOTHER.

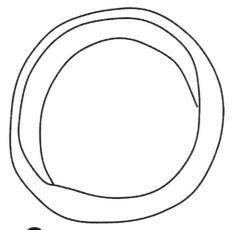

2 FORM A MOON-LIKE SHAPE INSIDE FIRST CIRCLE.

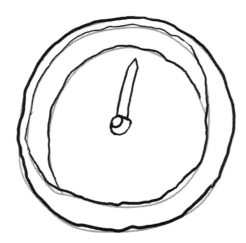

3 USE LINE GUIDES TO TRACE THE SHAPE OF THE COMPASS. DRAW THE NEEDLE OF THE COMPASS.

4 TO FINISH IT, DRAW SOME DETAILS AND ADD GLASS REFLECTION ON THE COMPASS.

Now, it's your turn

CAKE

DIFFICULTY LEVEL

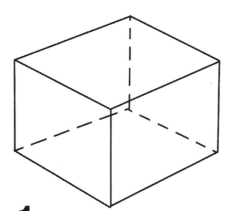

1 START WITH A CUBE.

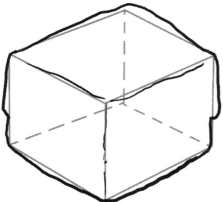

2 TRACE A SHAPE OF A CAKE.

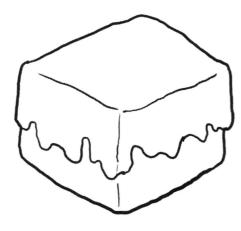

3 ERASE GUIDELINES AND DRAW A CREAM.

4 ALMOST DONE! DRAW SOME FROSTING AND SMALL DETAILS, AND YOUR CAKE IS DONE!

Now, it's your turn

SHEARS

DIFFICULTY LEVEL

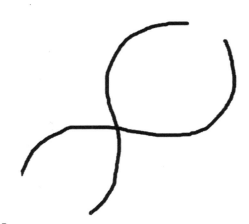

1 DRAW TWO WAVY LINES CROSSING EACH OTHER LIKE THE DRAWING ABOVE.

2 USE THE LINE GUIDES TO DRAW THE SHAPE OF THE SHEARS.

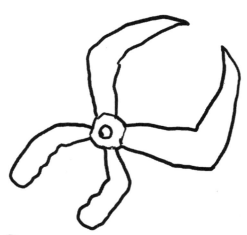

3 DRAW A JOINING SCREW AT THE CENTER OF THE SHEARS AND ERASE LINE GUIDES.

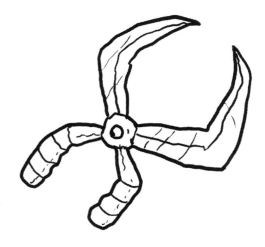

4 TO FINISH IT, ADD SOME DETAILS ON HANDLES AND BLADES.

Now, it's your turn

BED

DIFFICULTY LEVEL

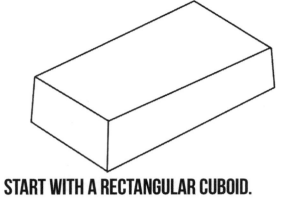

1 START WITH A RECTANGULAR CUBOID.

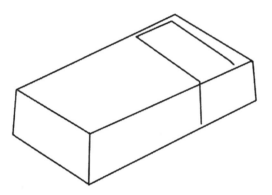

2 DIVIDE THE CUBOID INTO TWO PARTS.

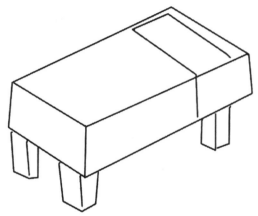

3 NEXT, DRAW THE FEET OF THE BED.

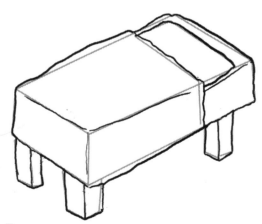

4 TRACE THE SHAPE OF THE BED AND REMOVE ALL THE LINE GUIDES.

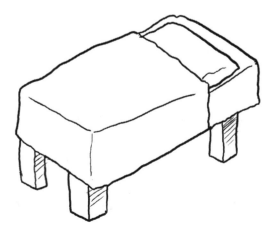

5 USE THIN LINES AND SHADINGS TO FINISH YOUR DRAWING.

Now, it's your turn

MAP

DIFFICULTY LEVEL

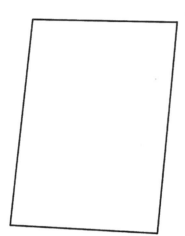

1 START WITH A RECTANGLE.

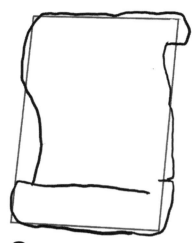

2 FOLLOW THE GUIDELINES AND TRACE A SHAPE OF THE MAP.

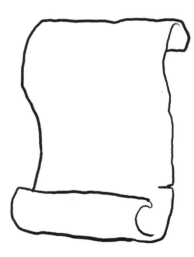

3 ERASE GUIDELINES AND DRAW WITH THICKER LINES THE FINAL SHAPE OF THE MAP

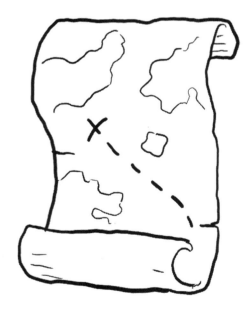

4 NOW, FINISH YOUR OWN MAP ANY WAY YOU LIKE!

Now, it's your turn

BOOK

DIFFICULTY LEVEL

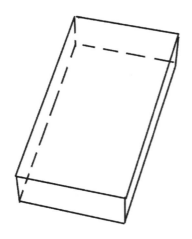

1 START WITH A RECTANGULAR CUBOID SHAPE.

2 FOLLOW THE SHAPE AND TRACE A SHAPE OF A BOOK.

3 ERASE GUIDELINES.

4 TO FINISH IT, DRAW SOME DETAILS ON THE BOOK COVERS.

Now, it's your turn

WHEAT

DIFFICULTY LEVEL

1 START WITH THIS FUNNY SHAPE.

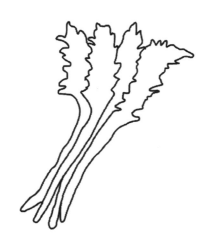

2 NOW, TRY TO COPY FIRST SHAPE AND DRAW SEVERAL OF THEM FORMING A BUSHEL.

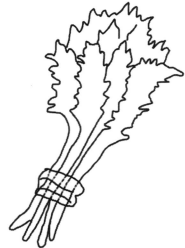

3 DRAW SOME MORE LEAVES ON TOP AND A CORD AROUND TWIGS.

4 TRACE OUR GUIDELINES AND DRAW A FINAL SHAPE OF WHEAT BUSHEL.

5 TO FINISH IT, USE THINNER LINES FOR SOME SMALL DETAILS AND SHADINGS.

Now, it's your turn

MINECART

DIFFICULTY LEVEL

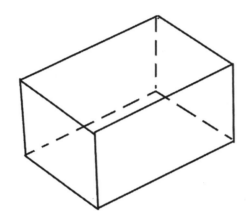

1 START WITH A RECTANGULAR CUBOID SHAPE .

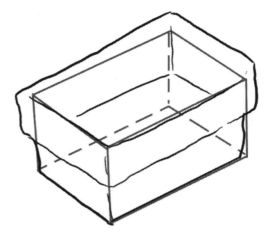

2 FORM THE SHAPE OF THE MINECART USING THE GUIDELINES.

3 ERASE GUIDELINES AND ADD WHEELS ON MINECART.

4 TO FINISH IT, ADD SOME DETAILS ON EDGES AND SHADINGS.

Now, it's your turn

PUMPKIN

DIFFICULTY LEVEL

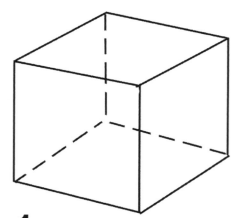

1 FIRST DRAW A CUBE.

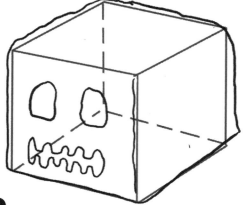

2 TRACE THE GUIDELINES AND DRAW A PUMPKIN SHAPE. ADD ITS EYES AND MOUTH,

3 ALMOST DONE, NOW YOU HAVE THE SHAPE OF THE PUMPKIN.

4 TO FINISH PUMPKIN, DRAW IT A PEDICEL AND SOME SHADINGS.

Now, it's your turn

TNT

DIFFICULTY LEVEL

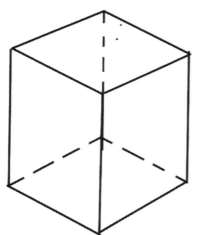

1 START WITH A LARGE CUBE.

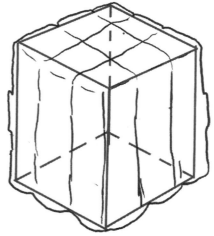

2 FOLLOW THE DRAWINGS ABOVE AND TRACE THE SHAPE OF THE TNT.

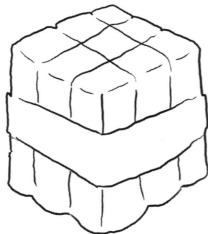

3 ERASE EXCESSIVE LINES AND DRAW THE LABEL FOR THE TNT.

4 WRITE TNT ON THE LABEL AND DRAW A FEW WICKS AND IT'S DONE.

DIFFICULTY LEVEL

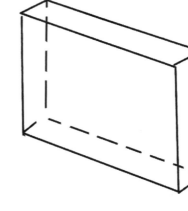

1 DRAW A FLAT RECTANGULAR CUBOID JUST LIKE IN OUR DRAWING.

2 DRAW A SMALL CUBE ON THE UPPER MIDDLE PART OF THE SIGN AND DRAW A LONG VERTICAL RECTANGULAR CUBOID BELOW THE SIGN.

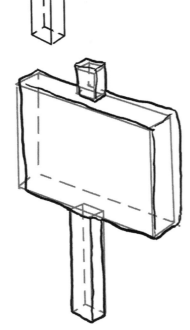

3 TRACE LINES TO DRAW THE FINAL SHAPE OF OUR SIGN.

4 DRAW SMALL DETAILS AND SHADING, AND WE HAVE SIGN!

Now, it's your turn

MUSHROOM

DIFFICULTY LEVEL

1 FOLLOW THE DRAWING AND START WITH THIS FUNNY LOOKING SHAPE.

2 DIVIDE THE SHAPE YOU MADE INTO THREE PARTS JUST LIKE THE DRAWING ABOVE.

3 ADD SPOTS ON IT TO MAKE IT LOOK MORE LIKE A MUSHROOM.

4 ALMOST DONE NOW! TO FINISH IT, DRAW SOME SMALL DETAILS.

Now, it's your turn

SPRUCE

DIFFICULTY LEVEL

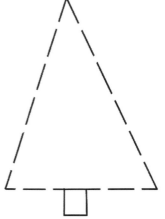

1 FIRST, DRAW A TRIANGLE WITH A SMALL SQUARE BELOW IT.

2 DRAW WAVY HORIZONTAL LINES ALONG THE SIDES OF THE TRIANGLE AND FORM THE SHAPE OF THE SPRUCE.

3 ERASE GUIDELINES AND USE THICKER LINES TO FORM THE SHAPE OF THE SPRUCE.

4 ADD SOME SMALL DETAILS, AND HERE IT IS!

Now, it's your turn